I wrote memorandums and things.
I indexed the letter-books too.
When the office-boy wasn't about.

And nothing could please me at night —
No novels, no poems, no plays,
Hardly the talk of my friends,
Hardly my hopes, my ambition.

I did as my desk-fellows did;
With a pipe and a tankard of beer,
In a music-hall, rancid and hot,
I lost my soul night after night.

It is better to lose one's soul.
Than never to stake it at all.

Some "artists" I met at the bar.
And others elsewhere; and, behold.
Here are the six I knew well.

I

MARY-JANE MACPHERSON

He thinks I'm a governess still.
But I'm sure that he'll pardon my choice;
I make more, and rest when I'm ill.
And it's only the sale of my voice.

I doubt it is sinful to dream;
The World's the true God-head, I fear;
Its wealth, power, iniquity seem
The mightiest Trinity here.

And this on a leaf of its book.
Which is life, and is ne'er out of date.
Is the passage I see when I look
As in Virgil for tidings of fate:

"You must each undergo a new birth;
You must die to the spirit, and be
A child of the lord of the earth.
Of our Saviour, Society.

"Get wisdom of worldly things.
And with all your getting, get gold;

Beware of the tempter who sings
Of other delights than are sold.

"But of all things a poor girl should shun,
It is the despising of pelf;
And another as notable one
Is the loving a lad like herself.

"Because while she dreams day and night
Of love, and good fortune, and bliss,
Oppression, disgrace, and despite.
Glad fiends that are never remiss,

"The world's evil angels of wrath
Pursue him she loves with their rods.
Till he falls overcome in the path;
For the World's the most jealous of gods."

Then I read in my heart, and I see
The heresy taught by my dear;
Before he was parted from me.
He whispered it into my ear:

"I go to make money, my sweet;
I'll join the gold-worshipping crew,
And soon bring the world to my feet.
For I'll worship and labour for you.

"Your work is to dream, dearest heart.
Of the happiest, happiest life."
I whispered, "I'll manage my part;
I'll dream day and night I'm your wife."

But that is so long, long ago.
Such daily eternities since;
And dreaming is sinful, I know,
And age all my poor darling wins.

Time patiently weaves from his sands
My life, a miraculous rope:
I would sever the cord in his hands
And die; but I hope, and I hope.

II

TOM JENKS

In a Music Hall & Other Poems by John Davidson

John Davidson was born at Barrhead, East Renfrewshire on 11th April 1857.

In 1862 his family moved to Greenock and there he began his education at Highlanders' Academy. Davidson would now spend many years at school and the beginnings of a career in various industries before gaining employment in various schools.

By now literature was a large part of his activities and his first published work was 'Bruce, A Chronicle Play' in 1886. Four other plays quickly followed including the somewhat brilliant pantomimic 'Scaramouch in Naxos' (1889).

With his reputation gradually providing an income he was also able to explore his true medium; Verse. 'In a Music Hall and Other Poems' (1891) together with 'Fleet Street Eclogues' (1893) were ample proof that he possessed a quite rare, genuine and distinctive poetic gift.

Davidson now turned further and further towards verse. In 1894 he published his most popular volume, 'Ballads and Songs' (1894), and this was followed by a further 'Fleet Street Eclogues' (Second Series) (1896) and by 'New Ballads' (1897) and 'The Last Ballad' (1899).

As the new century dawned Davidson was hard at work on a series of 'Testaments', in which he gave definite expression to his philosophy and were published over a seven year period; 'The Testament of a Vivisector' (1901), 'The Testament of a Man Forbid' (1901), 'The Testament of an Empire Builder' (1902), and 'The Testament of John Davidson' (1908).

However, on 23rd March 1909, with his finances in ruins, the onset of cancer and profound hopelessness and clinical depression he left his house for the last time. His body was only found on September 18th by some local fishermen.

Index of Contents

IN A MUSIC-HALL

Who is my neighbour?
Luke X. 29.

PROLOGUE

In Glasgow, in 'Eighty-four,
I worked as a junior clerk;
My masters I never could please.
But they tried me a while at the desk.

From ten in the morning till six

A fur-collared coat and a stick and a ring,
And a chimney-pot hat to the side — that's me!
I'm a music-hall singer that never could sing;
I'm a sort of a fellow like that, do you see?

I go pretty high in my line, I believe,
Which is comic, and commonplace, too, maybe.
I was once a job-lot, though, and didn't receive
The lowest price paid in the biz., do you see?

For I never could get the right hang of the trade;
So the managers wrote at my name, "D.B.,"
In the guide-books they keep of our business and grade,
Which means — you'll allow me — damned bad, do you see?

But a sort of a kind of a pluck that's mine
Despised any place save the top of the tree.
I needed some rubbing before I could shine.
Some grinding, and pruning, and that, do you see?

So I practised my entrance — a kind of half-moon.
With a flourishing stride and a bow to a T,
And the bark and the yelp at the end of the tune,
The principal things in my biz., do you see?

Oh, it's business that does it, and blow all the rest!
The singers ain't in it alongside of me;
They trust to their voices, but I know what's best —
Smart business, like clockwork and all, do you see?

I'm jolly, and sober, and fond of my wile;
And she and the kids, they're as happy as me,
I was once in a draper's; but this kind of life
Gives a fellow more time to himself, do you see?

III

LILY DALE

She's thirty, this feminine cove.
And she looks it at hand, you'll allow.
I was once on the streets. By Jove,
I was handsomer then than now.

Thin lips? Oh, you bet! and deep lines.
So I powder and paint as you see;
And that's belladonna that shines

Where a dingier light ought to be.

But I'm plump, and my legs — do you doubt me? —
You'll see when I go on the stage!
And there isn't a pad, sir, about me;
I'm a proper good girl for my age!

I can't sing a bit, I can't shout;
But I go through my songs with a birr;
And I always contrive to bring out
The meaning that tickles you, sir.

They were written for me; they're the rage;
They're the plainest, the wildest, the slyest;
For I find on the music-hall stage.
That that kind of song goes the highest.

So I give it them hot, with a glance
Like the crack of a whip — oh, it stings!
And a still, fiery smile, and a dance
That indicates naughtiest things.

And I like it. It isn't the best:
There are nurses, and nuns, and good wives;
But life's pretty much of a jest,
And you can't very well lead two lives.

But sometimes wild eyes will grow tame,
And a voice have a tone — ah, you men! —
And a beard please me — oh, there's my name!
Well? I take a week's holiday then.

IV

STANLEY TRAFFORD

This of me may well be said —
Of a host as well as me:
"He held himself as great; he made
His genius his own protégé."

I loved the beauteous star-veiled truth,
I strove and failed, and strove again.
I wrote some verses in my youth.
And knew two noted poets then.

Now I wear a tinsel dress,

Now I strum a gilt guitar;
For I made my first success
As "The Sentimental Star."

I could be more glad than most,
I was born for happiness.
Since despair began to boast.
No one ever tasted less.

The sun, the stars, the moon, the sea —
I say no word of these — a sign,
A little good sufficed for me,
A rose's scent made heaven mine.

But most some old thing newly thought
By some fresh thinker pleased my sense,
And strong, sweet words with rapture wrought.
And tempered with intelligence.

I craved not wealth, I craved not fame,
Not even a home; but only time
To dream the willing dreams that came.
And keep their record in a rhyme.

Wherefore I starved, and hither fell,
A star in this the nether heaven.
Without, I shine; within, is hell.
What might have been had I still striven,

Had I not sold my soul for bread!
But what is this? I'm dull to-night;
My heart has quite seduced my head;
I'm talking poetry outright.

Ha, ha! I'll sing my famous song,
I feel I can recall its tone;
The boy's dream suits the gas-lit throng!
Mark — "Words and music all my own."

And then, oh, then! Houp-la! Just so!
Selene, Lily, Mary-Jane?
With which, I wonder, shall I go
And drown it all in bad champagne?

V

SELENE EDEN

My dearest lovers know me not;
I hide my life and soul from sight;
I conquer all whose blood is hot;
My mystery is my mail of might

I had a troupe who danced with me:
I veiled myself from head to foot;
My girls were nude as they dared be;
They sang a chorus, I was mute.

But now I fill the widest stage
Alone, unveiled, without a song;
And still with mystery I engage
The aching senses of the throng.

A dark-blue vest with stars of gold,
My only diamond in my hair,
An Indian scarf about me rolled:
That is the dress I always wear.

And first the sensuous music whets
The lustful crowd; the dim-lit room
Recalls delights, recalls regrets;
And then I enter in the gloom.

I glide, I trip, I run, I spin,
Lapped in the lime-light's aureole.
Hushed are the voices, hushed the din,
I see men's eyes like glowing coal.

My loosened scarf in odours drenched
Showers keener hints of sensual bliss;
The music swoons, the light is quenched.
Into the dark I blow a kiss.

Then, like a long wave rolling home.
The music gathers speed and sound;
I, dancing, am the music's foam,
And wilder, fleeter, higher bound.

And fling my feet above my head;
The light grows, none aside may glance;
Crimson and amber, green and red.
In blinding baths of these I dance.

And soft, and sweet, and calm, my face
Looks pure as unsunned chastity.

Even in the whirling triple pace:
That is my conquering mystery.

VI

JULIAN ARAGON

Ha, ha, ha! ho, ho, ho! hee, hee, hique!
I'm the famous Californian Comique!
I'm as supple as a willow.
And as graceful as a billow,
I'm handsome, and Tm strong, and I've got cheek.

Cheek's nothing; no, by Jingo! I'm obscene!
My gestures, not my words, say what I mean
And the simple and the good.
They would hiss me if they could,
But I conquer all volition where I'm seen.

I twist, contort, distort, and rage and rustle;
I constrain my every limb and every muscle.
I'm limber, I'm Antæan,
I chant the devil's pæan,
I fill the stage with rich infernal bustle.

I spin, and whirl, and thunder on the board;
My heart is in my business, I'm encored;
Tm as easy as a sprite,
For I study day and night,
I dream, devise — I travail, by the lord!

"My nature's a perennial somersault,"
So you say, and so I think; but whose the fault?
If I don't know good from evil.
Is it wrong to be a devil?
You don't get lime-juice cordial out of malt.

But I'm plump, and soft, and strong, and tall, and sleek.
And I pocket twenty guineas every week;
I journey up and down,
I've sweethearts in each town,
I'm the famous Californian Comique.

EPILOGUE

Under the earth are the dead.

Alive and asleep; overhead
Are the angels, asleep and dead.

Not even shadows are we,
But the visions these dreamers see.

These dreamers below and above —
The dream of their dreams is love.

But we never will count the cost;
As dreams go, lusty and stout.
We make us a heaven and hell.

There are six dreams I knew well;
When I had sung them out,
I recovered my soul that was lost.

POEMS (1872-89)

The pieces are not arranged in the order of composition.

WINTER IN STRATH EARN

She crumbled the brown bread, she crumbled the white;
The snow lay deep, but the crumbs lay light:
The sparrows swept down like withered leaves;
The starlings sidled with scarlet greaves.
And burnished, black-green harness scrolled
With damaskings of dark old gold;
The gallant robin, he came not nigh.
But a tom-tit sparkled a frightened eye;
The blue blackbird with his saffron bill
Hopped with the crowd; and the finches sped
With their scarves of white and their vests of red
From the sea-green laurels; and out of the hill,
Where the steep Blue-rocks stood, stark and gray,
A jackdaw flew; and the carrion crow
Frightened them now and again away.
Swooping down on the bloodless prey
All in the powdery snow-white snow.

She crumbled the brown bread, she crumbled the white.
She fed them morning, noon, and night.
They fought and scolded till supper was done.
Then wing after wing went away with the sun.

The twinkling Earn, like a blade in the snow.
The low hills scalloped against the high.
The high hills leaping upon the low.
And the amber wine in the cup of the sky.
With the white world creaming over the rim,
She watched; and a keen aroma rose,
Embodied, a star above the snows;
For when the west sky-edge grows dim,
When lights are silver and shades are brown,
Behind Torlum the sun goes down;
And from Glenartney, night by night.
The full fair star of evening creeps;
Though spectral branches clasp it tight,
Like magic from their hold it leaps.
And reaches heaven at once. Her sight
Gathers the star, and in her eyes
She meekly wears heaven's fairest prize.

ALICE

The paynims seized her in the wood
Where shadows moved alive,
Where steep rocks made a well of shade,
And no sweet flowers might thrive.

One from her hair the pearl-strings tore:
She seemed as fair again;
The pearls, the only gems she wore.
Lost all their lustre then.

A cry she cried: "Help, help, dear love!"
They gagged her with her lace;
Her scarf — white silk, like foaming milk —
They bound across her face.

Pale, dumb with lust, they rent her robes;
She thanked God for her hair.
White in the wood, unsheathed she stood,
The only flower there.

But when she felt her nakedness,
These wolves she clasped and clang;
Their eyes devoured her sweet distress,
And low their laughter rung.

The ruthless paynims then cast lots
Who should possess her first.
"Hark, Alice! hist! I keep my tryst!"
And in her lover burst.

He fought the three, and felled each foe,
That none should ever rise;
Then stood. She loosed her scarf; and lo.
Their souls were in their eyes.

Right as her quickened spirit rose
Her shuddering body dawned;
Her arms would veil the tinted snows.
Her sight restore its bond,

But shame, the body's false friend, died —
Flame in the sun's clear frown:
Only her virgin soul he eyed;
Her arms hung meekly down.

He leapt the space between; her eyes
Held his with trembling power.
No word they spoke; wrapped in his cloak,
He bore her to her bower.

THE GLEEMAN

The gleeman sang in the market-town;
The market-folk went up and down.

His blue eyes waned when thronging thought
Would not obey as visions ought;
Then flashed and flung their radiance straight-
Availing prayer — at heaven's gate;
And thought and word chimed with the tune.
His scarlet cloak and sandal shoon,
His tunic with the silver fur,
Of forest green and minever,
His golden brooch and carcanet,
Was not the garb that gleemen get.
So said the dames; the dreamy girls
Gazed only on his golden curls;
The sapless ancients sneered and frowned;
The young men with a spell were bound,
And eyed his gleaming, studded belt,
The scabbard and the jewelled hilt.

But no one praised the harp of gold
His fingers deftly rang.
Or listened to the things he told;
But this is what he sang:

"Loose your knotted brains awhile,
Market- people, sore bested;
Traffic palsies all your isle;
Hear a message from the dead.

"Though the sultry flood of life
Brims my veins; though starry truth
Still maintains a changing strife
With the purple dreams of youth;

"Songs the master-makers wrought —
Who are now the guests of death,
Lulled by echoes of their thought —
Fill me with their eager breath.

"What! You stare with horny eyes,
And my singing-robes you scan?
You would make my sword your prize?
Maidens only see the man?

"Learnèd clerk with icy sneer.
Must I strike a lower clef?
Hear, O heaven, and earth, give ear,
I will sing though men be deaf I

"And the throbbing sky shall list.
And the rivers cease to bound,
Startled mountains pierce the mist,
Happy valleys drink the sound.

"Earth is fairer than we know:
Shining hours and golden beams!
Lilies sigh, and roses glow.
And the beasts have noble dreams.

"Lo! the youngest soul is scarred.
Blanched with tears and dyed with stains.
For the world is evil-starred.
But the vision still remains:

"Plenty, from her bounteous horn,
Dealing bread instead of stones;

Golden lands of nodding corn
Lusty labour reaps and owns;

"Fearless suns, and no sick star.
No more maiden moons ashamed,
Cities sweet as forests are.
Sin unthought, unknown, unnamed;

"Babes that wail not in the night.
Wretched heirs of poisoned lives;
No young souls that long for light.
Festering in scholastic gyves;

"Not a damsel made the tomb
Of a thousand loves unchaste;
Woman mistress of her womb,
Never bound to be embraced;

"Man by hunger unsubdued.
Conqueror of the primal curse,
Master of his subtlest mood.
Master of the universe."

He wrapped his cloak about his face,
And left the bustling market-place.
The juggler had an audience,
The mountebank drew showers of pence,
The pardoner cheapened heaven for gold
I ween the market-folk were sold.

FROM GRUB STREET

RONDEAU

My love, my wife, three months ago
I joined the fight in London town.
I haven't conquered yet, you know,
And friends are few, and hope is low;
Far off I see the shining crown.

Pm daunted, dear; but blow on blow
With ebbing force I strike, and so
I am not felled and trodden down.
My love, my wife!

I wonder when the tide will flow,

Sir Oracle cease saying "No,"
And Fortune smile away her frown.
Well, while I swim I cannot drown;
And while we sleep the harvests grow,
My love, my wife.

ROUNDEL

My darling boys, heaven help you both!
Now in your happy time of toys
Am I to die? How I am loth,
My darling boys!

My heart is strong for woes or joys;
My soul and body keep their troth,
One in a love no clasping cloys.

Why with me is the world so wroth?
What fiend at night my work destroys?
Has fate against me sworn an oath,
My darling boys?

VILLANELLE

On her hand she leans her head.
By the banks of the busy Clyde;
Our two little boys are in bed.

The pitiful tears are shed;
She has nobody by her side;
On her hand she leans her head.

I should be working; instead
I dream of my sorrowful bride,
And our two little boys in bed.

Were it well if we four were dead?
The grave at least is wide.
On her hand she leans her head.

She stares at the embers red;
She dashes the tears aside,
And kisses our boys in bed.

"God, give us our daily bread;
Nothing we ask beside."
On her hand she leans her head;
Our two little boys are in bed.

THE REV. HABAKKUK MCGRUTHER

A battle-cry for every session
In these wild-whirling, heaving last days:
"Discard for ever the Confession;
Abolish, if you choose, the Fast-days;
Let Bible knowledge in school and college
No more be taught — we'll say, 'All's well.'
Twill scarcely grieve us, if you but leave us
For Scotland's use, in Heaven's name. Hell."

NOCTURNE

The wind is astir in the town;
It wanders the street like a ghost
In a catacomb's labyrinth lost.
Seeking a path to the heath.
Broad lightnings stream silently down
On the silent city beneath.
But haunting my ear is the tune
Of the larks as they bathe in the light;
And I have a vision of noon
Like a fresco limned on the night:
I see a green crescent of trees;
A slope of ripe wheat is its foil.
The cream of the sap of the soil,
Curdling, but sweet, in the breeze.
The sun hastes, and evening longs
For the moon to follow after;
And my thought has the tenderest scope
Tears that are happy as laughter,
Sighs that are sweeter than songs,
Memories dearer than hope.

THOMAS THE RHYMER

"Thomas the Rhymer .... had said to a great Scotch nobleman, called the Earl of March, that the sixteenth day of March should be the stormiest day that ever was witnessed in Scotland. The day came, and was remarkably clear, mild, and temperate. But while they were all laughing at Thomas the Rhymer, on account of his false prophecy, an express brought the news of the king's death. 'There,' said Thomas, 'that is the storm which I meant; and there was never tempest which will bring more ill-luck to Scotland."
— Tales of a Grandfather.

Home from the wedding of the king
The earl rode late and soon.
A wizard's strain sang in his brain;
And in the afternoon
He met the wizard by the sea —
Thomas of Ercildoune.

"And this," said then the scornful earl,
"This is your stormiest day!
The clouds that drift across the lift
Are soft and silver-grey;
One sail, too near to be a bird,
Glides o'er to Norroway.

"A blush is on the weather-gleam,
The sun sinks low and lower;
The gloaming fills the cup he spills,
The faint moon bending o'er;
The sleepy waves, reluctant, poised.
Drop peacefully ashore."

The elfin lord of Ercildoune,
That weary wizard, said:
"Tell me, I pray, what chanced that day
The King of Scots was wed.
An uninvited bridal guest.
They say, came from the dead."

"They truly tell. The king led forth
His bride to head the dance;
And in her mood fair maidenhood
Had summoned every lance
Of nameless, gracious witchery,
Of matchless smile and glance,

"For one last conquest of mankind.
A shout rang to the roof;
Each star-bright eye shone eagerly
To weave the viewless woof
Of airy motion through the warp
Of music. Swift reproof

"Fell on us; for a soundless wind
Blew purple every light;
The dancing ceased; the dancers clasped
Each other's hands; each knight
Before his trembling lady stood.
Blanched, breathless, at the sight.

"An odour, chill, sepulchral, spread.
And lo, a skeleton!
A creaking stack of bones as black
As peat! It seemed to con
Each face with yawning eyeless holes,
And in a breath 'twas gone."

Three times aloud laughed Ercildoune,
He laughed a woeful laugh.
"A sign!" he cried. "Say not I lied
Till night-fall." With his staff
He wrought grotesquely in the air.
Then said: "Our land must quaff

"The bitterest potion nations drink;
This token is the last.
Recall, my lord, the weltering horde
Of loathly worms that passed
Northward, and like a filthy sponge
Wiped greenness off as fast

"As west winds wash the snow; that orb
That shook its spear of awe
Beside the brand Orion's hand
Is still in act to draw,
A hideous star — these eyes of mine
Its glare at noonday saw;

"The floods that swamped flocks, fields, and towns.
While men in throngs were slain;
Earthquakes that took the land and shook
The meads beneath the main —
Shells gleamed by drenched flowers, tangle clung
Like snakes about the grain:

"Herewith strange fire from heaven fell,
Mayhap for priestly crimes.
On abbeys fair; the hinds still stare.
And mutter saving rhymes.
At belfries in fantastic heaps

Resoldered by their chimes.

"I rede these signs to mean a storm:
That storm shall break to-day/'
With face on flame a rider came.
"It's herald, by my fay!"
The Rhymer said, and sudden swept
His robe and beard away.

Said then the panting messenger
"The King of Scots is dead!"
The earl grew white. "The King! — Alight."
But he rode on ahead.
"The heir's a baby over seas:
In truth are we stormstead!"

ANSELM AND BIANCA

Even in her passion's lofty tide.
When nothing seemed too hard to dare.
When earth's most lowly lot, her pride
With Anselm had been proud to share,
A shadow started at her side,
A ghostly whisper clove the air,

Down fluttered dead her high-flown dream.
When Anselm hoarsely pled: "Be mine!"
"No, no!" she answered. "Though I seem
To have no thought that is not thine,
I dare not wed. I sadly deem
Marriage for us is death's dark shrine."

And looking like the twilight skies.
That now unbosom, now conceal
Their meaning stars in rhythmic sighs.
She made his anguished being feel
Love's keenest pain, saying, with closed eyes:
"Beseech me not; my senses reel."

A time there came when Anselm ceased.
Save by his looks that helpless pled.
To urge her. Then her love increased
As pity deepened; nameless dread
Had prisoned love; but love, released.
Grew free and fearless as the dead.

"Make me your bride, and if," she said,
"Our wedding day be Doomsday, then
We'll end time now." So they were wed.
Even as she wished, that day. And when
Homeward Anselm Bianca led.
Trees seemed to her as walking men:

Her bridal vision far outran
The swiftest sight of mighty seers:
She failed to note time's dainty span,
But saw the day beyond the years.
And highest God, the shadow of man.
And man, the image of his fears.

And like a little child she thought:
"If all the world had only dared
To seize the pleasure that it sought,
Earth had been heaven." And Anselm shared
Her mystic mood: their souls had caught.
As souls that have in hell despaired.

Or souls that have in heaven hoped,
Catch ever that green ray revealed
Only to who have soared or groped. . . .
The wedding-bells panted and pealed
Like happy hearts; and evening coped
A monumental day love built.

Night's monogram, the twilight star,
In silver wrought upon the hem
Of pallid gold that flickered far —
The border of the sky — for them
Throbbed like two passionate flowers that are
Lit in one bloom on one fair stem.

Their hearts the only music made,
Until their golden ringing felt
The dulcet, lowly serenade
That lowly friendship sweetly dealt
For gentle dealing. "Love," she said,
"Speak, or my happy eyes will melt!

"Say if you like the music, sir."
She blushed like one that is too bold.
"Yes, very well," he answered her.
"My love," she said, "I have been told
Music is like Arabian myrrh,
That yields what scent the senses hold."

"Or like a diamond," Anselm mused.
"From rippling notes a desperate mind
Draws sweeter sadness; mirth is fused
To liquid smiles; and lovers find
Their ladies' words; the latch is loosed
Of heaven's gate, and saints made blind.

"The tune breaks forth in showers of light,
But one beam strikes each listener's sense.
Oh, sweetheart, could we hear aright
The deep tone, shy as Proteus, whence
Melodious sound takes birth, more bright.
More vital than this hour intense,

"Our future would appear." "And we
How much the wiser? Ah! I fear
To see the future, love, would be
Only a vision of our bier."
She said this quaintly. Archly, he:
"What is your meaning? Let me hear."

I mean were we our last hour told,
Though day to day, like rhyme to rhyme,
Re-echoed joy — an age of gold —
Death, like a hideous gifted mime,
Would haunt us, dumb with meaning, bold.
Careless as one who knows his time.

So not to know is better, dear,
That knowledge that we must disown.
Let us not talk of death. "What? Here!
My love!" But on the instant blown,
A strident note crashed through the clear
And tinkling music, like a stone

Breaking the murmur of a stream;
And after came the trumpeter,
A herald, with plume of foaming cream,
And stood before them. "Noble sir,
Prince Florio sends me, and my theme
Is recompense. Deliver her.

"Your bride, to him." "A monstrous jest!"
"An old jest, sir, from death's jest-book.
'Your father, Anselm, was the best
Who ever played it, when he took
Prince Florio's mother, and the rest

From lord to knave, drowned in the brook,

"That hissed with blazing beams, and frothed
About the burning tower." "He seized
His own true wife, to him betrothed.
But rapt away." "My lord was pleased
To bid me hold no words." "This loathed,
Unfellowed insult! What! Appeased

"By just my bride! You — hellish one! —
Tell him — unworthy to be man—
Your lord, I'll strip him, in the sun.
And whip him dead." "My master's plan
To do as by his sire was done
Is well" "Away! "The herald ran.

Bianca sobbed: "Where shall we fly?"
"Nowhither, love; we'll fight. Be still.
Be patient, pray." Her fearful eye
Clung to him piteously, till
She stood alone; then sigh on sigh
Like incense rose; and on the sill

Of life her soul beheld the soul
Of destiny. "Then this it was,"
She thought, "that did our talk control
Deathward. When most without a cause
They seem, our thoughts leap at the goal.
Merciful God, bid horror pause!"

Anselm returned, white as the dead
"Take all your jewels. Bravely, dear!
Our festal friends, our men — all fled!
The tower's besieged; but do not fear:
The stair within the wall will stead.
Be quick! I'll help you, love." "Hush! Hear!

"They beat the gate!" "One afternoon —
Listen — (I travelled years ago
In Italy) — I heard a tune,
And thought to see a boy; but, lo!
Rounding a knoll, I Lighted soon
Upon an ancient, lying low

"Beneath a wild vine, clustered ripe.
I laughed to scorn the pastoral.
He nodded, fingering his pipe;
Then said: 'There is no life at all

But love: so after many a stripe
Deserved and undeserved, I call

"With music back my love, my youth.
My spring, my summer burnt to ash –
Which is the sifted soul of truth –
I sit without the din and crash
Of drudging life; and memory's tooth
Bites golden apples.' This was trash,

"But now the old man's steady gaze
Across the blue lake, bossed with isles,
The green and golden slopes, the haze
That veiled with purple serried files
Of snow-capped mountains, and the ways
That crawled through flowers, and leapt the stiles,

"Are balm to me. That lake's our bourne.
Come, love, sweet love." He spoke no more;
For having touched the spring to turn
The quaintly graven, secret door.
Hidden behind a curtained urn
That came from Tuscany, a roar

Of fierce, exulting voices burst,
With iron tread and armour's clang,
Out of the opened wall. And first
He kissed her; then his bright sword rang
Scabbardless, and he stood. None durst
Approach his guard until he sprang

Upon them. Two foes fell; then, he.
He staggered to his feet, and bled,
Leaning against the wall. But she.
Haled from before her unpressed bed
At which she knelt, strained to be free,
And "Save me, save me!" hoarsely said.

Back surged his life; that breath of woe
Summoned it back. He made one stride.
Shook free his eyes, and saw his foe
With sword advanced before his bride.
He rushed upon the steel — even so!
And plunged his own deep in her side.

I, John Auld, in my garret here,
In Sauchiehall Street, Glasgow, write,
Or scribble, for my writing-gear
Is sadly worn: a dirty white
My ink is watered to; and quite
Splay-footed is my pen — the handle
Bitten into a brush; my light.
Half of a ha'penny tallow-candle.

A little fire is in the grate.
Between the dusty bars, all red —
All black above: the proper state
To last until I go to bed.
I have a night-cap on my head.
And one smokes in a tumbler by me:
Since heart and brain are nearly dead.
Who would these comforters deny me?

Ghosts lurk about the glimmering room,
And scarce-heard whispers hoarsely fall:
I fear no more the rustling gloom,
Nor shadows moving on the wall;
For I have met at church and stall,
In streets and roads, in graveyards dreary,
The quick and dead, and know them all:
Nor sight nor sound can make me eerie.

Midnight rang out an hour ago;
Gone is the traffic in the street,
Or deadened by the cloak of snow
The gallant north casts at the feet
Of merry Christmas, as is meet;
With icicles the gutter bristles;
The wind that blows now slack, now fleet,
In every muffled chimney whistles.

I'll draw the blind and shut — alas!
No shutters here! . . . My waning sight
Sees through the naked window pass
A vision. Far within the night
A rough-cast cottage, creamy white,
With drooping eaves that need no gutters,
Flashes its bronze thatch in the light.
And flaps its old-style, sea-green shutters.

There I was born. . . . I'll turn my back;
I would not see my boyhood's days:

When later scenes my memories track.
Into the magic pane I'll gaze.
Hillo! the genial film of haze
Is globed and streaming on my tumbler:
It's getting cold; but this I'll praise.
Though I'm a universal grumbler.

Now, here's a health to rich and poor,
To lords and to the common flock.
To priests, and prigs, and — to be sure! —
Drink to yourself, old Ayrshire Jock;
And here's to rhyme, my stock and rock;
And though you've played me many a plisky,
And had me in the prisoners' dock,
Here's my respects t'ye, Scottish whisky!

That's good! To get this golden juice
I starve myself and go threadbare.
What matter though my life be loose?
Few know me now, and fewer care.
Like many another lad from Ayr —
This is a fact, and all may know it —
And many a Scotchman everywhere,
Whisky and Burns made me a poet.

Just as the penny dreadfuls make
The 'prentice rob his master's till,
Ploughboys their honest work forsake,
Inspired by Robert Burns. They swill
Whisky like him, and rhyme; but still
Success attends on imitation
Of faults alone: to drink a gill
Is easier than to stir a nation.

They drink, and write their senseless rhymes,
Tagged echoes of the lad of Kyle,
In mongrel Scotch; didactic times
In Englishing our Scottish style
Have yet but scotched it: in a while
Our bonny dialects may fade hence:
And who will dare to coin a smile
At those who grieve for their decadence?

These rhymesters end in scavenging.
Or carrying coals, or breaking stones;
But I am of a stronger wing.
And never racked my brains or bones.
I rhymed in English, catching tones

From Shelley and his great successors;
Then in reply to written groans.
There came kind letters from professors.

With these, and names of lords as well,
My patrons, I brought out my book;
And — here's my secret — sold, and sell
The same from door to door. I look
My age; and yet, since I forsook
Ploughing for poetry, my income
Comes from my book, by hook or crook;
So I have found the muses winsome.

That last rhyme's bad, the pun is worse;
But still the fact remains the same:
My book puts money in my purse,
Although it never brought me fame.
I once desired to make a name.
But hawking daily an edition
Of one's own poetry would tame
The very loftiest ambition.

Ah! here's my magic looking-glass!
Against the panes night visions throng.
Lo! there again I see it pass,
My boyhood! Ugh! The kettle's song
Is pleasanter, so I'll prolong
The night an hour yet. Soul and body!
There's surely nothing very wrong
In one more glass of whisky toddy!

THE SWING

We sat on the swing together;
At the end of the orchard-close,
A hill with its budding heather
Like a purple dome arose.

On the heavily-ivied chapel
The sun for the windows sought;
In the shadows of pear-tree and apple
The daisies were crowded and caught.

And this was her thirteenth summer,
And I was as old as she;
But love is an early comer;

He came to her and me.

O, silently, slowly swinging,
Till a star peered half afraid.
And the chapel-bell was ringing,
And the shadows were lost in shade!

THE TRIUMPH OF LOVE

"Love, your love — speak low —
Now, give it now to me.
Your pride? Let it go, let it go.
Your wealth? Let it sink in the sea.
Women like you should be poor;
Gold upon beauty is vain:
Love, O lady, be sure
Is loveless without some pain.
Let the triumph of love be seen;
Come poor to me, poor, my queen."

The lady rose at length.
And looked to earth and sky;
She laughed in her loving strength,
And flung her bracelets by;
She scattered her wealth abroad.
She donned a homespun gown.
And said, as she took the road:
"Now, sweetheart, we shall go down
Where poverty reigns as queen.
That the triumph of love may be seen."

"WHEN THE WAYS WITH MAY-FLOWER WHITEN"

"When the ways with May-flower whiten,
And before the lilac blooms,
When the songs and feathers brighten
In the forest's bridal rooms;
Though your beauty should forsake you.
And your love itself decay,
I will come, my own, to take you,
If I have to fight my way."

So her heart at peace reposes
Till the winter-time shall go;

But the lilac and the roses,
And the fruit came, and the snow;
And the years came, and age took her;
All her beauty did decay;
For her lover false forsook her;
But her love shall last for aye.

IS LOVE WORTH LEARNING?

Is it worth the learning,
This love they praise?
Pale lovers yearning
For happy days,
For happy days and happier nights.
For waking dreams of dear delights?
Is it worth the learning?

My heart is burning.
It scorches me;
Is it worth the learning
What this may be?
Why do I walk alone all day?
"She is in love," the maidens say.
Is love worth learning?

Was it worth the learning?
He kissed my hand.
Is love worth learning?
I understand,
Though love may come and love may go,
It is the only thing to know:
Love's worth the learning.

THE NAIAD

The Naiad sings within her well:
"My waves are crystal clear;
My voice is like a tinkling bell;
My banks are never sere.

"I comb my rippling locks of gold.
And then with violets blue
I twine a wreath their braids to hold,
Some fashion, quaint and new.

"Each little blue flower-universe
That nestles in my hair,
Enskies a thousand dewy spheres;
Each sphere, a rainbow fair.

"My grotto in the sweltering noon
Is cool as tongue can tell;
I sing all day my naiad-rune,
And tend my bubbling well.

"And when the sun at eventide
Has loosed his fiery yoke,
I haste to dance in meads unspied
With other fairy folk."

THE MALE COQUETTE

I have a heart; pray, do not go,
Sweet ladies, all and some.
It beats for you "Plan-plan!" for, lo,
'Tis hollow as a drum!

Behold my soft and softening eyes!
The fading star of morn
Hangs not so sweetly in the skies:
Why blaze yours then with scorn?

My tongue drops honey like a hive;
My hands are soft and small.
What! I am only five feet five!
Well, some are not so tall.

Look at the diamonds on my breast,
My golden chain and locket,
My many suits, all of the best —
And never mind my pocket

Pathetic songs of love I sing,
And you may have your choice:
I play; I flash my diamond ring;
Falsetto is my voice.

I tread a higher walk of art
Than he who plights his troth,
Then breaks it, and the maiden's heart:

Such clumsy work I loathe.

A gold and silver mine for me
Is every blooming maid;
With tongue and eye I work, and she
Scarce feels the pick and spade.

To strike a tender, golden vein,
And draw it from the eyes
In glowing glances; with a chain
Of welded words and sighs

To raise a blush upon the face;
Or with dynamic power
Explode the thought's most hidden place;
And at the parting hour

To gain a little fluttering sigh:
These are my art's high aims;
And in its practice I will die
In spite of nasty names.

A male coquette? Well, be it so:
The pig delights in dirt.
The poet in his verses' flow;
And I was born to flirt.

CHEOPS

Osiris, Apis, Isis, gods indeed!
Their temples have been closed since I was crowned,
And still the sun and moon their journeys speed,
And that fat, crescent-fronted bull has found
The goad stronger than god, if he be that.
Now am I king, powerful as liberty
From counsel, law, religion, can estate
The monarch of the mightiest monarchy
While life is mine: there is the filthy fly
That spoils my dainty dish — Cheops must die.

And shall I then inhabit bird or beast?
I'd be a bird to live a life on high;
Of dew to drink, on luscious fruit to feast;
Some splendid, noble bird — the Phoenix, I!
In Araby the blest my home shall be,
Where balmy winds caress each spicy grove.

And dally sweetly with the smiling sea.
Where all the elements are linked in love.

There shall my shining crest and beauteous neck
Of purple feathers gemmed with golden ones.
My snow-white tail with here and there a fleck
Like evening crimson, and my seeing suns
Flash on the blue of heaven when noon is bright,
And gleam a gorgeous spectre in the night,
The wonder of the world, the theme of seers.
For countless leases of a thousand years.

Methinks I'd sooner be a beast or bird
Than enter once again a human frame;
For spirits are in human flesh interred
Not wedded unto strength, or winged with flame:
And use and wont, fate's angels, have disposed
Even of Cheops' life, though less than more:
But wherefore should there be on me imposed
One subtle bond; wherefore should I deplore
A thought unproved, a wish ungratified,
Because of anything to be defied?
Why should I sympathise at all with men?
The world and its inhabitants exist
For kings alone: to use my chattels then.
Clogging humanity being thus dismissed.

The race of men hath issued none knows where.
Even like a locust-cloud in harvest-time;
And when its pasture, earth, is nibbled bare,
It shall fare someward to some unknown clime.
The greater part of time to gain the less
Men spend in toil and sleep, two kinds of death,
And momentarily their lives possess
In feeding, laughing, breeding; not in breath.
Each generation passes, living, dying,
And thinks itself somewhat — yea, so much worth,
That the successive ages magnifying
The individual life have seen far forth
To a mirage of immortality,
Imaged from life's lasting reality.

O foolish men who think yourselves so great.
Ye are but fires that burn a little bout.
And being used to mould some toy by fate.
Transmit your flames, then go for ever out.
Proud-blooded men, I'll teach you what ye are;
I'll stop your spring-like health, and blast your flowers;

I'll set your petty happiness ajar;
Ye shall no more have any happy hours:
I will be fate, and ye shall be my jests.
Things merely to fulfil all my behests.
Ye shall be lashed to work, and worked to death
At labour neither beautiful nor good.
Useful, good, beautiful? — these words are breath.
And all is vanity. Hold firm my mood.
And Egypt that believes itself so wise.
Shall bear the cost and sorely agonise.
To rear avowedly what now it makes
Unwittingly, huge nothing,

(Whereupon he planned a pyramid)

WOOD IN AUTUMN

I wandered in a wood upon a day
In ripe October, and the corn was reaped.
Beyond the mossy boles in fair array
The builded heaves appeared, in sunlight steeped;
Their drooping ears no gentlest wind assailed;
Each long, rough shadow reached the other's
On some dark stake they seemed to be impaled,
Or strung like beads the sloping field to grace,
Behind them through the trees the reddening west,
But faintly blushing yet, told to the world
The time was coming on it loves the best,
When to its deeps the warm sun should be hurled.

All suddenly the silence of the wood,
Then only by the insects' humming broken,
With wailing was fulfilled even as I stood,
No motion made they as a warning token;
But each tall tree and bush that rooted there,
Shook, to a breath of its own breathing trembling;
For each had found a tongue, and on the air.
Without artistic flourish or dissembling.
But simply from its core sent forth a song.
All in the burden joining tunefully,
Whenas the thorn with voice that echoed long.
Had sung a verse of that sad melody.
The dark and secret pine beat time to them;
The strong old oak took up a mighty bass;
The mountain-ash and beech with fluted stem
Warbled the tenor; and the treble's place,

Besides the thorn, the gentle birch fulfilled;
While all the saplings sang an alto strong.
Making such harmony I was well- willed
To listen ever to that greenwood song.

I knew the meaning of the sounds they sang
Then as I listened; but when they were done.
There did about my aching memory hang
A sounding echo, all the meaning gone.
Whether they mourned their tarnished, ragged dress.
Fast leaving them with bare, unsheltered backs.
Or for their long-lost Hamadryades,
Or comrades fallen before the woodman's axe.
Or other still more lamentable thing,
I know not; only this, I heard them sing.

A SAIL

The boat was pearl, the mast was gold
And fretted with diamond-stone;
The sail was blue, of the azure hue,
And silk of the finest tone.

The gold gave forth a golden sheen,
The diamonds like suns gleamed bright,
And the silken sail shone as it had been
Woven of starry light,
And the glow of the pearl was like the glow
Of the moon in a summer night

Beyond the range of the elfin lights,
Over all a midnight gloom
Fearfully hung like a darkness sent
From the place of eternal doom;
But round the boat the sea shone fair,
Fair as a sunny sky;
And the channels between the islets green
Like rainbow strips did lie.

The isles were surely isles of the blest:
Luxuriance hid the soil;
Each fairer than Eden seemed.
Each brighter than heaven beamed;
And the beings who bore the moil
Were fairy creatures whose joyous features
Seemed to know nothing of toil.

They brought us food, and they brought us wine
From the Edens all around;
The food of the gods and their nectarous drink
Were never more luscious found.

Among the trees, along the shores,
And within the silken sail,
A nameless wind sweet-smelling blew
A long, voluptuous wail.

The boat slid on like a sledge on ice;
The lights they never grew dim;
The wind ever blew, and the fairy crew
Had never a weary limb.

O softly, slowly, swingingly
Along the serpentine sea!
Between the isles for miles on miles.
And ever more merrily!

On purple cushions of taffeta
With tassels of golden thread,
Beneath a canopy of silk
My sweetheart laid her head;
And I scarce could tell where her bright hair fell,
Which was the hair or the thread.

She lay in a robe of gossamer,
So fine that her gentle limbs
Shone through the white, and gave it a tint
As delicate as e'er was lent
To the rose-leaves' waxy rims;
And through her lashes her dark eyes shone
Like the diamonds upon the mast;
And her bosom was bare, and the charmed air
Made a music in it with her flowing hair.
And mine shook with a passionate blast.

FOR LOVERS

When in the morning I awaken first,
I find your head upon my shoulder laid.
Its clustered wealth of golden treasure burst
Forth of the band wherewith 'tis nightly stayed.
I hear the swallows twittering in their nest

In our wide-open, southern window hung,
And eke the lark, tired out with love and rest,
Shouting that song he has so often sung;
And many a lusty cock crows long and loud;
The languid, strolling breeze into our room
Flings stolen sweets from every flower and bud,
Easing his heavy burden of perfume.
Anon your eyes heave up their skyey lids
Welling with dawn; my raptured gazing bids
A blush auroral to your bright cheek speed,
A smile breaks forth, and it is day indeed.

Then forth to spend the pleasant summer day
That holds such infinite, supreme delight.
It makes us blame the sun's most lengthened stay
In summer's noon, and curse the scowling night,
Even as we pouted at the early beams
That darkened dismally our loving dreams.

Along the brown, crisp, withered woodland way
Bestrewn with greenest moss and maiden-hair,
That like an aisle's thick matting winding lay
Between the trees that pillar the blue air,
Hand clasped in hand and voice attuned to voice,
chanting in borrowed words our own true love
With such divine, enraptured, Sapphic noise
As stills to listen blackbird, merle, and dove,
And with a tread heart-lightened to such ease
As would have added grace to Dian's bearing,
With eyes that lighten, locks free to the breeze,
Two waves of love, full-breasted, onward faring,
Through all the wood and swift across the lea
We hurry downward to the happy sea,
And cast ourselves on ocean's boundless stream.
Even as we have been flung into time's dream.
We lie and listen to the hissing waves,
Wherein our boat seems sharpening its keel,
Which on the sea's face all unthankful graves
An arrowed scratch as with a tool of steel.
We gaze right up into the simple blue,
We watch the wheeling, diving, sailing mew.
Oh then, we think if ever on our love
Vulture calamity shall flap his wing.
We will not wait until we have been hove
Half-eaten to despair, that wolfish thing;
But while our eyes are yet undimmed with tears,
And ere hope's ague has become quotidian.
We will forestall despair and blighting fears,

Sheltering in death our love's unstooped meridian:
For in our boat even at the sun's midnoon,
Like two discoverers we will straight embark,
And sail within his shadow, that bright boon,
A voyage parallel to his great arc.
And then in his red, western winding-sheet
Sink down with him to death's rest, deep and sweet.

Then in our naked godhood hand in hand
Into the joyous element we spring:
So light we are, thereon we almost stand,
But the sea clings us like a living thing.
And you are lovely swimming in the sea.
And like a creature born and bred therein;
But never did a thing so fair and free
Inhabit there, nor ever shall, I ween.
I bear you on my back a little way;
For meed you sing an ocean melody.
So sweetly in the splendour of the day
That all the rippling waves move silently;
And round about the air intensely listens,
And from his pride an eagle stoops to hear,
The sun your face with all his wonder glistens
And earth stands still; eternity is near;
Amazèd eyes of fish through ocean's wrinkles
Peer out like scattered stars in noon of night;
Not air; nor bird breathes note, no wavelet tinkles;
All nature is death-still to hear aright.

Enrobed again we set our sails for shore,
And having landed, in an arbour dine.
Then forth we bound — scarce half the day is o'er
Our restless spirits more elate with wine,
We listen to the mowers' cheery song;
We laugh at clownish, soul-less labourers,
And shout upon the dead to come along
And leave their filthy shrouds and sepulchres.
Through narrow field-paths, threading close-ranked
And tasselled oats, and heavy-scented beans,
And beadsmen barley in obeisance meet
Sloping their cowlèd heads before the means
Of life in everything, the mighty sun;
Along rough roads where sweet wild roses blow
To-day in pomp, to-morrow dead and done;
Where in the ill-dug ditches cresses grow;
By hedges that have been unbarbered long;
Across a bridge the Romans built of yore
The river's banks buttressing, 'tis so strong,

With ancient ivy wholly mantled o'er,
We stray. You gather as we pass along
Wheat-ears, and barley-ears, and tinted vetches;
Wild rose-buds that the nightingale's sweet song
Ne'er listen to full-blown, for — beauteous wretches! —
The sun's kiss that the scent rapes from their breasts
And opes their blushing bosoms, kills them too;
Bride-bed of gnats, woodbine, that hedges vests;
Forget-me-nots, scarce as your eyes so blue;
A lone spring primrose waning now in June
As Hesper pales when onward comes the moon;
And little earnest daisies, single-eyed.
That worship heaven with faces glorified.
With fairy fingers than the flowers more fragrant
This spoil of fields you link into a chain;
On shaggy rocks with groping foot and vagrant,
I search for berries and a hatful gain.
With berries crushed we make ourselves shame-faced;
With berries pierced you string a grassy thread;
Then with your flower -wove chain I gird your waist,
And wreathe your flower-outshining, golden head.
And on my knees fall down and worship Thee,
My berry-stained, flower-crowned deity!

While from the very highest heaven of song,
And highest welkin-height a wing has measured,
Relays of larks their love-songs loud prolong
In surging notes that are in heaven treasured.
And then each quick descends from heaven's height;
His spirit swoons in such a high-pitched flight;
His serviceable wings, his tongue of fire.
His sun-enduring eyes wax faint and tire.
Where in the universe then must he wend?
Why, to that clime where languid poets use,
His mate's sweet bosom — she, his only muse,
As I to you my wearied spirit bend.
And drink deep draughts from those sweet fountains twin.
Your eyes, Castalia and Hippocrene.

Within a pool, deep in a pebbly strand.
The purest of the diamonds that are strung
Upon the glen, a bracelet of the land.
We see the heavens as in a mirror hung.
Oh, then we wonder upon what great loom
The warp and woof of heaven's tent were wrought!
Who reared its poles and gave such spacious room,
Who hung its deathless lamps, their bright fire brought?
I wonder at your beauty's perfectness;

I wonder at the blueness of the sky;
I wonder at the sun's bright steadfastness;
I wonder at the breeze that wanders by;
I wonder at the larks constantly singing,
And at the proper motion of the stream;
I wonder at the still, green grass up-springing.
And what sweet wonder fills your sweet day-dream;
I hear the rolling music of the spheres,
Wondering, and wondering at the cloven dell;
I wonder at the floating gossameres;
I see creation is a miracle.

We climb a hill, and there behold the sun
Sink down aglow with work serenely done.
And while we watch his orb fast disappearing,
Lo, from behind us like a sable sprite,
A lonely crow sails past, right sunward steering,
A seeming, silent pioneer of night;
Down the ravine a screaming curlew flies;
We are transfigured by the crimson skies.

Night comes and brings its honey-laden hours;
The pillaging wind flies with its scented spoil
Up from the robbed and sweetly moaning flowers;
Your silk hair nets it in a golden toil;
Love's night recedes, and love's day nearer lowers;
Love is the world's life-blood, and you and I
Two pulses throbbing in one melody.

Hark, from afar the corn-crake's mellowed call
Hush, in the grove the nightingale is singing!
The stars throb last as they to earth would fall,
In their inwoven spheres love's music ringing.
Subdued almost, our sense can hardly tell
The music from the odour; it perceives
A sweetly-scented tune, a sweet-toned smell;
Love mingles everything its soul receives.
Lo, you and I with God are all alone,
And you and I with Him will now be one.

A MAY MORNING

A distant cock crows loud and clear;
The larks are singing loftily;
The cloudless sun his noon is near;
A southern wind blows o'er the lea.

On every grass-green blade is hung
The morning's diamond dewy order;
The shadows of the hills are flung
Head-foremost o'er the river's border.

The river flows with stately ease;
The high-heaved firmament of blue —
Does it reflect the azure seas.
Or do the waters take its hue?

The dells are rich with primroses;
The leas are white with snow of daisies;
And every streamlet's rim knows this —
It soon will win love's dearest praises.

For ever the waves seem murmuring,
"When are you coming, blue flowery skies?
When will you shine on us here while we sing.
Sweetly shine with your sunny eyes?

"Are you lighting the fairies' gloomy grots.
Delicate, fairy chandeliers?
Where are you shining, forget-me-nots?
When are you coming to dry our tears? "

"Summer is coming," the bee is humming,
Humming with honey-sweet hum
That sweetens the air, for summer is coming —
Coming! — the summer is come!

THOREAU

I tell you who mock my behaviour,
There is not a desert in space;
I Each insect and moss is a saviour,
And Nature is one thing with Grace.

Who called me a hermit misprized me;
I never renounced a desire;
The thought of the world has disguised me,
And clad with a vapour my fire.

But soon in the night of my dying
The pillar of cloud will be lit,
And the dark world, ashamed of its lying.

Behold I am fairer than it.

"He is terrible; no one can love him;
His virtue is bloodless and cold;
He thinks there is no soul above him;
His birthright it was to be old."

O scandalous worldling, self-centred,
Can you love what you cannot descry
With a vision the light never entered?
Is your conscience less dreadful than I?

Close-sucking the bone and the marrow
Where life is the sweetest, I fed
Like an eagle, while you, like a sparrow.
Hop, hunting the streets for your bread.

As freshly as at the beginning,
The earth in green garments arrayed.
In the dance of the universe spinning,
A pregnant, immaculate maid,

Looks up with her forehead of mountains,
And shakes the pine-scent from her hair,
And laughs with the voice of her fountains,
A pagan, as savage as fair.

DECEMBER

The heartless, sapless, dying year
With icy fingers
Clutches the earth in mortal fear;
And while life lingers

Within his veins that swelled with spring,
And glowed with summer.
And now are poisoned by the sting
Of that old-comer,

Who comes to all to end their days,
Whom men call Death,
He breathes upon the earth's wan face
His chilly breath.

If it may be to strike her dead
For company;

To die alone he is afraid;
And some there be

Of men and flowers as old and frail.
With blood as sere,
And some both young and sweet, as pale
As is the year,

Who will be buried in the snow
With him to sleep;
Their souls came from and now must go
To the unknown deep.

But those whose lives are dwelling still
In lively frames
Are full of mirth, and take their fill
Of works and games:

Make love, make wealth, gain fame, gain power.
As if for ever.
Forget that life is but an hour,
A sea-bound river,

And warm with sport laugh at the cold;
Yet is it true
If they live long they will grow old —
I mean not you;

Not you, nor me: we only know
Our blood is fire
Can melt the longest winter's snow,
And not expire.

THE VOICE

When it comes like a levin-brand
You must not evade the voice;
Die manfully where you stand,
But receive the shaft of its choice.

It is this that now blinds my soul's sight:
We are motes in a ray of God's eye;
But he knows not we dance in his light,
He is blind as the sun in the sky.

It is this that now slaughters my soul:

We are not worth damning to hell,
Or rewarding with heaven. That's the whole
Harsh word of the voice from the well.

What star shines there in the gloom?
Who speaks? Is it God? Is it I?
Who shouts through the trumpet of doom?
"It's a lie, it's a damnable lie!"

BETROTHED

He
Betrothed to one who loves me dearly,
Who is the most enskyed lady
In sight of every wild and staid eye.
That knows her body's beauty merely.

Yet is delight a dead thing to me;
She whom I worshipped now I love not;
I am worse than dead if death will move not
To save me while it does undo me.

And she is fairer, stronger, vaguer.
Than any perfect, splendid statue
That looks in neutral marble at you:
She has no soul within to plague her.

And she is sweeter than the portrait
Of any tender, sweet Venetian,
Painted in deathless tints by Titian;
But she is dead — surely a sore trait!

I looked; and lo, her wondrous beauty!
I loved; and lo, she glowed with passion!
I reached to heaven; she clung to fashion;
She is its queen; I, slave to duty.

She was still-born; death nursed her, fed her;
She is a miracle that's common,
A lovely, loveless, soulless woman:
The world's sepulchral palace bred her.

She loves me? Well, wants to be mated.
Married? I must be married to her.
She will not see what, were I truer
She should be told, that I am sated

With all her divers ways of pleasing;
Yea, of her very beauty too, sick
As one who tires of verse or music,
And bound to keep my ache increasing.

She
He loved me once, but now he's feigning.
I loved him not when most I thought it;
But from his passing fire I caught it:
Now like the moon's my fire is waning.

I would have one whose love would seize me,
Light me, inspire me, put life in me.
And from the mouldy dead world win me.
He loves me not; he shall release me!

ON A HILL-TOP

The airy larks ceased shouting in the lift
With fearless voice pitched at the utmost height.
Attendants of the sun, the steadfast, swift,
And mighty hunter of the thronging night.
What time a wanderer from a mountain-crest
Beheld the mist-hung, crimson- lighted west.

A hectic village — pleasure's summer daughter —
A bay with boats, a frith most like a lake,
With ruby stain spilled on the hither water,
And on the further, shade in mass and flake.
Between the mountain and the mountains lay
Unseen by him. His eye's enchanted ray

Burnished the sunset with a melting glance
Of more ethereal fire, that leapt along
The serried summits like the golden lancc
The cloudy champion, thundering, flings among
The huddled, quaking hills. The west obeyed
The summons of his eye, and quick repaid

His gift of added splendour, opening wide
The gate between the two eternities.
Forth issued first a streaming billowy tide
Of dulcet music as of psalteries.
Crested with fierier sound; with it broke out
Flushes of throbbing colour like the shout

Of people newly freed, with trumpets, gongs.
Drums, clarions — their hues so pulsed and lived;
From far within there floated gusts of songs
Sung by sweet voices. Then his soul received
In that baptismal flood of resonant light
And luminous sound the gift of second-sight.

Dreams are the blossoms borne by rooted thought;
And visions watched by mightiest seers have been
Bright shades of meditative fancies caught
On some midnights immaculate, black screen;
But he beheld his lady in the sky;
And all the heroes whom he loved passed by.

They issued shadowy from the glowing door,
And swept like regal clouds with lofty gait,
Bending before her. On the azure floor
Enthroned she sat in sweet and solemn state
Above both day and night, where time is heard
Singing soft snatches like a far-perched bird.

"MAKE ME A RHYME TO STARLIGHT"

Your eyebrows are indistinct,
But your eyes are the kindliest gray;
They are wells of fire and dew,
The marriage of April and May,
Laughter and tears interlinked.

Your brow is lowly and true;
Your hair is dusky and gold;
Your lips are curved and red.
And soft and warm, and they fold
A flock of the pearliest hue.

When passion had made you its bed —
A flame waking up in a lamp —
Through the mist of the world like a far light,
You beaconed me forth from the damp,
Dark life, where I lay as one dead.

Of all heavenly creatures that are bright,
Your spirit's the noblest and purest;
And your voice, which is love sublimed.
Is the slowest to speak but the surest.

And as piercing and soft as the starlight;
And that last's the rhyme you wish rhymed.

KINNOULL HILL

We sat on the verge of the steep
In a coign where the east wind failed.
In heaven's top, cradled, asleep,
The young sun basked, and deep
Into space the universe sailed.

And eastward the cliff rose higher,
And westward it sloped to the town,
That smoked like a smouldering fire
Built close about spire after spire;
And the smoke was pale-blue and brown.

The smell of the turf and the pine
Wound home to our heart's warm core;
And we knew by a secret sign
That earth is your mother and mine;
And we loved each other the more.

And out of the rock, scarred and bare.
The daws came crying in crowds,
And tossed themselves into the air,
And flew up and down, here and there.
And cast flying shadows, like clouds.

We heard not the lark, but we heard
The mellow, ineffable tune
Of a sweet-piping, wood-haunting bird.
Our heart-strings were stricken and stirred.
And we two were happy that noon.

THE MAHDI

Islam is living! Follow me,
God's champion against the world!
A new crusade time shall not see;
But lo, our battle-flag unfurled!

The pestilence shall stalk about,
And fleet-winged Azrael shrilly sing:

The heavens shall hang their meteors out
And streams of blood in deserts spring.

Shetan's chief slave shall lead a host;
And Gog and Magog issue forth:
A grisly smoke, hell's swartest boast.
Shall coil about the stifled earth.

God's wrath burns like a desert when
Harmattan blows: to quench its heat
From adamantine hearts of men
Our scimitars a fount shall beat.

Our counsel shall be swift and wise;
Our motion shall be mystery;
Death-shafts shall dart forth of our eyes
From victory to victory.

Then shall the great Archangel blow
The trump of doom, and at the sound
The shrivelled rivers cease to flow.
And ocean's bed be naked ground.

A second blast; and like a light
Blown by a wind the sun shall stream
And wither out; and in that night
The heavens shall vanish as a dream.

A spectral silence, felt, unknown,
Shall haunt the weltering chaos, till,
With bloodless cheeks, and trembling tone,
Wet eyes, sad heart, and feeble will,

The angel faintly blow again:
Yet Adam in his grave shall hear;
The deepest dead shall rise amain;
And hell and paradise appear.

The terrors of the dread abyss,
The shrieking throngs by demons lashed
Over the brink with fiery hiss,
We shall behold, awed, unabashed,

A moment. Then our happy feet
Along the keen and star-bright thread,
Al-sirat's filmy bridge shall fleet;
And sure shall be our feathery tread.

Mohammed beckons at the gate!
Up, follow me in ways he trod!
The languid, green-robed houris wait!
Hear, and obey the word of God

So here I have by happy chance
A rambling tower of Babel,
A crow-stepped, roof-bent, rough-cast manse
With fruit on every gable.

My glebe is fifty acres round,
And there my corn is growing;
My poultry cluck with cosy sound;
I hear my cattle lowing.

Above the plane-trees, gray and high
My solid steeple rises;
It looms between me and the sky
Like other earthly prizes.

But I have clear and without fail,
Or trust in harvest's ripe end
For fiars' prices, on the nail.
Five hundred pounds of stipend:

And naught to do, the truth to speak,
Save sit and sip my toddy,
And write a sermon once a week,
And bury anybody.

Some half-a-dozen marriages
Come in the pairing season;
I visit sick folk if they please —
Or anything in reason.

The world is here some ages late,
And stagnant as a marsh:
I thank my stars it is my fate
To have a country parish;

For wearing done with constant use
For me has no inducement.
And city charges play the deuce
With all a man's amusement.

The sheep are few: somehow to God
I'll answer how I fed mine . . .
And there's my gallant salmon-rod.
And there my famous red-line.

With these last autumn on the Earn
I killed the thirty-pounder
That seemed amid the lapping fern
No glossier, nor rounder,

Than cased in glass it looks there — see,
Beneath my gun and pipe-rack —
The gun the earl presented me,
My seasoned pipes, a ripe stack.

My single life contents me yet;
I have some oats to scatter:
A barmaid or a ballet-pet
Is no such deadly matter.

When one is on the sunny side
Of thirty and an athlete:
At thirty-five I'll take a bride,
And make the narrow path meet.

As many a man has done before.
The broad one: it will lead me
To live in health and see fourscore.
And have my son succeed me.

NO MAN'S LAND

As I do live, these things I tell
Are true and written with my hand. —
Like Lucifer from heaven I fell,
And dropped at night in No Man's Land.
My feet took root in shifting sand.
Whose grains were broken bones of men;
But from that ghastly grinding strand
I writhed my body free again.

I came upon a grove of fir,
And found a coney-paven street
Which led where scented juniper
Did hedge an arbour warm and sweet,

For goddesses' appointments meet.
There were old roses, autumn-proof,
And violets sleeping at my feet.
And woven woodbine made the roof.

Sleep wound me in her purple zone,
And laid me on a bed of moss
Like dark green taffeta that's sewn
With golden lace of rusted gloss.
No need had I to turn and toss:
I slumbered like a babe new-born;
But knew the moon had struck across
My head when I awoke at morn.

I dipped my face among the dew;
The rosy odours were my food;
I knelt where valley-lilies blew,
And agates all the channel strewed,
To drink with birds; I was endued
With power to understand their notes;
They lauded love as lovers should,
With eager hearts and trembling throats.

As through the wood I took my way
They flew along from tree to tree,
And cheered me with their roundelay;
And I was glad as I could be.
But when I heard the moaning sea,
And reached the forest's bourn, they fled,
An empty heaven overhead.

And straightway then I understood
That it was evening; half an hour
Had seemed my journey through the wood.
And yet a day had passed; the bower,
The birds, the time were in the power
Of some enchantment, as I thought;
I wondered whose could be the dower
Of witchcraft that this thing had wrought.

Soon I was ware who wove the spell:
There stood between me and the west
That burned with sunset, on the swell
Of the high lea, a woman, dressed
In crimson, with a golden vest;
A crescent crown, with jewels proud,
Among her hair, half-loose, half-tressed.
Sat like a rainbow on a cloud.

Her head upon her shoulder hung,
As she undid her hair; one arm
Was naked; to herself she sung:
And that is how she works her charm
On souls of men to do them harm.
I shook, and shrieking would have gone.
But natheless all my soul's alarm.
With her bright eyes she drew me on.

Low, low she laughed and kissed my mouth,
Then wrapped me in her golden hair.
She was a sorceress in sooth,
And held me with a mother's care
Close to her bosom pressed; and there
Her strong heart did the charm conclude,
Entuning mine until it bare
A burden to her beating blood.

She took me to a curtained cave,
Where lamps, like moonlight, white and still.
Shed perfumed lustre. The bright wave
That furthest dares when great thoughts fill
The ocean's heart of love, and spill
In swelling tides, stole up and laid
One kiss upon the cavern's sill,
Then shrank away as if afraid.

At moments music, soft and rich,
From hidden minstrels came in gusts;
Anon the rainbow-crested witch
Sang piercing songs of loves and lusts;
And once she spake: "Behold where rusts
The armour of an elfin knight!
Behold! with thrice three deadly thrusts
I killed him: he defied my might."

Night sank: the moon hung o'er the wave,
But such a radiant flood was thrown
Across the waters from the cave,
The moon was like a ghost — her own;
No palest star beside her shone;
And pageants through that bright sea-room
Whose heaven-high walls were night, swept on
From gloom to glare, from glare to gloom.

I saw the ocean fairies float;
And Venus and her island passed;

I saw Ulysses in his boat —
His struggles bent the seasoned mast.
I, too, prayed madly to be cast
Among the waves, when close in-shore

The Syrens, singing, came at last;
But the witch wove her spell once more.
I saw a ship become a wrack;
Charybdis laughed, and Scylla bayed;
Arion on the dolphin's back.
By Nereids courted, sang and played;
And Proteus like a phantom strayed;
Old Neptune passed with locks of white;
When Dian came, the heavenly maid,
I saw the moon had vanished quite.

Then voices rose and trumpets rolled;
And broidered, silken sails appeared,
And crowded decks, and masts of gold,
And heavy, blazoned banners reared —
The burning eye, the swarthy beard.
The glittering arms with gems inlaid.
The starry swords the Paynim feared.
The glory of the first crusade.

Straight came a storm; from thunder-clouds
The golden lightning streamed and flashed.
And fired the twisted, silken shrouds.
And gilt the foam; the thunder crashed,
And rain like arrows stung and lashed
The pallid knights, whose armour rang;
Ship smote on straining ship and thrashed
The waves, and shrill the wild wind sang.

Then suddenly the sun arose.
And from her cave she made me pack.
That wanton witch, with gibes and blows,
I prayed her to be taken back
And see more visions, when — alack! —
Fast rooted in the grinding strand
I found myself, the human wrack,
The ghastly verge of No Man's Land.

JOHN BALIOL AT STRATHCATHRO

A gorgeous flourish as of victory,

And Baliol entered, vested like a king.
Crowned, sceptred, almost looking like a king.
Before went portly mace-bearers; behind
His son came first, and then the Constable
Bearing the sword of state; and after him
A train of shamed and sullen ministers.
"What pageantry is this?" King Edward cried.
"Rather what mockery?" said Annandale.
But Baliol, heeding not, spake solemnly:
"My sovereign liege, high peers, and friends and foes,
I come to do my kingly obsequies.
A royal spirit did inflate my life
Which' I mistook for an attendant sprite
With me incorporate when Norway's maid,
A wan, cold pearl, the hungry sea received
To glimmer in its unsearched treasure-house.

This genius first embraced me when a boy:
High manners of command among my mates
Seemed warnings of what fate was wooing me.
Our feudal households all are little courts;
But in the regiment and discipline
Of my retainers and my family
There did exist a true monarchial style
More perfect than the Scottish Court could boast.
Thus ever entertained I kingly state,
And loved it chastely, unexpectantly;
And when I was made king my heart was glad.
But oh! the tarnished and inglorious crown
Proved triple what are all kings' diadems,
A thorny torment, and no fortune-cap.
Lo! when I walked between two holy men
To be anointed in the holy place,
Even as an infant's first supported steps
Start it upon its journey to the tomb.
So then began with me this sorry end.
An infant has a king within itself,
Whose fleshy vesture as it wears, grows fair
To perfect manhood; thence sweet, mellowing age
Ripens it on to hoary majesty;
The which thrown off, forth steps the kingly soul.
The veiled informer of the graceful flesh.
But I, when I have doffed my kingly dress,
Disgraced and ugly shall be all-despised."
King Edward here broke in on him, and said:
"An histrionic king! What say you, lords,
Shall he speak on, or go out sighing now?"
The Earl of Annandale took up the sneer:

"Nay, let him speak, while memory prompts his tongue:
I warrant it was practised in a glass!"
But Baliol-like a stag at bay replied:
"Lord Annandale, your taunt is envy-bred.
Remember when you stand, as I stand now.
Which very well may chance, how I resigned
My majesty, and imitating me,
Worthily do a most unworthy deed."
"The unworthiest deed was to accept a crown
Which was not yours." But Edward cried: "No more!
You come, Lord Baliol, to resign the crown,
The kingdom, your ill-government has wrecked."
"The rocks I struck upon were English rocks
Alluring with false beacons. Macers, come,
Lay down these clubs; they have beat out my eyes."
Then stepping forward to Lord Annandale,
"Proud Earl, this is the sceptre; scan it well.
It is of silver; lo! a lovely stalk
All barked about with gold. It blossoms, too.
Like Aaron's rod; look, there are fleurs-de-lis;
And here are thistles of rare workmanship;
And images of sacramental cups;
Medusa-heads that strike each other dead;
Hours could be spent in following this foliage
Winding and intertwining: see, three knobs
Divide the shaft: it is a candlestick,
And from its capital there rises out
A taper, clasped and held by imaged saints.
Ending and flaming in a crystal ball:
Alas! it only lit my own dark shame.
A kingly sceptre, a magician's wand,
Powerful and subtle! So I hoped: it made
A double ell of weakness in my hand:
It was my wife, but ne'er possessed by me;
So now I yield it wholly to that priest
Who made me cuckold as he married us,"
And slow at Edward's feet he laid it down.
Then taking off his crown the weary king
His sad apostrophes began again.
"The crown imperial, a splendid gem!
Thy weight shall never more oppress my brow.
I coveted thy gold-knit jewel- walls,
And for a day delighted me in thee
When thou becam'st the palace of my brain.
I scan thy triple rampire wonderingly;
Thy fair, broad base, so rich with varied stones.
Look at these slabs of oriental pearl.
These topazes, and amethysts and rubies,

And hyacinths, and emeralds, and garnets.
Shining like faces in their golden collars!
Look at them, lords! they gleam like very suns;
Your eyes like moons do borrow of their fire,
And flash it back, giving and taking lights
With all the wistful eagerness of love.
Sapphires and diamonds form the second storey,
And twenty golden turrets tipped with pearl:
In them too there's a syren witchery
Of singing, gentle sighing, snaring scent.
Fair crosses, flowered of pearls and diamond dust,
Build up the third cirque; and from it four arcs,
Curiously chased and figured, meet and close.
Enamelled blue and powdered o'er with stars.
Crowned with a cross. The walls are softly hung
With tire of purple velvet, diamond-laced.
Alas! my lords, this noble gorgeous dome
My head has found a blank immuring jail;
Its velvet tire like sackcloth flayed my brows.
And on its cross my soul was crucified.
Here, take the crown." King Edward took it up
And put it on, saying: "I will wear it too."
Then Baliol, reaching out a trembling hand:
"Give me the sword. Shall I unsheathe it? There;
Five feet of steel panged full of angry fire,
And tempered to a mood most murderous.
Give it a bloody scabbard, shall I now.
Within your bosom, king? That were a deed!

I am no doer. Back into thy bed,
Thy dainty crimson-curtained resting-place,
A lair too lovely for so fierce a brute:
I lay it at your feet, not in your heart."
King Edward girt him with a sword, and said:
"Thou art as sure a madman as a fool."
"Madmen are sometimes simply overwise;
All men are fools, yea, very full of folly;
Folly is ignorance, and every soul
Can have of knowledge such a little share,
Omniscience sees a gross and foolish world;
The greatest fool is he who cannot know.
Adversity has taught me many things;
I am content to be a fool and mad."
"That last was sensible: I like you now."
He heeded not, but doffed his robe and said:
"Off purple dress! I cast thee from me here
With hundredfold the joy I did thee on.
Methinks the martyr, tortured, wrenched, and broke,

From his torn mortal garb escapes at last
To find less ease than now my being feels.
The seal! the seal! Lord Chancellor, the seal!
So; now I sign my own enfranchisement:
The kingly slave is now a noble freeman;
Now I'll betake me to some decent life."
Then up King Edward rose and took his turn.
"Tarry a little. Think you that our power
Defied and now triumphant will endure
To pass unpunished your rebellion?
This your submission is most politic.
But you must not depart hence unrebuked.
Sir William Ormesby, we commission you
To write a paper of this Earl's transgressions;
His weakness and his folly; his French league.
Set down therein that he acknowledges
The perfect justness of our present war;
And that he sorrows deeply for his crimes;
And begs not pardon, merciless to justice,
But humbly for such sentence as may please
Our injured and insulted sovereignty.
This shall he read armed with a snowy wand.
The mocking baton of black criminals.
Before our deputy and all the peers:
Which being finished, shall in part atone;
And for the rest, imprisonment of him
And of his son while it shall be our will."
"Alas! I see submission, mild and meek,
Turning when one is struck the other cheek,
But rouses ire in heartless dignities,
Who batter mouth, brow, and beseeching eyes.
I gave up all, and having nothing, lo.
The nothing that I had is stolen so! "
Then soldiers led him and his son away,
While Annandale to Edward softly said:
"My liege, I think you promised me a crown;"
And got for answer, loud and mockingly,
"Good Earl, think you that we have nought to do
But conquer crowns, and hand them o'er to you?"

THE QUEEN OF THULE

The Queen of Thule loved a lord
As poor as poor could be:
Her people pled with her to wed
The Prince of Orcadie.

She thought her strength of love at length
Would make their wishes fade;
And night by night the lovers met
Deep in a forest-glade.

A streamlet like a wind-blown lyre
Now paused, now murmured soft;
The moon came like a lily on fire
With love, and watched them oft

She played eaves-dropper to their talk;
From heaven she bent her head,
And in her star-attended walk
She pondered what they said.

Why is the Queen alone to-night?
"Come, come," she cries, "to me.
O wind, breathe low! — 'Tis Harold! — No;
The Prince of Orcadie!

"What brings you here?" "A pliant fate
Puts you into my hand;
So yield you now: Heaven knows my vow
To rule you and your land."

"You told me that you loved me, sir;
And sure it made me rue
That you must pine; for love of mine
Can never be for you.

Sir, you must leave me." "Thus, alone?
That were a gentle deed!"
"What make you here?" "I chased the deer
All day upon my steed.

"Three dark brown hinds I killed, and then —
My heart still pants withal —
I killed a gallant stag of ten:
His horns may grace your hall."

"I like you not, dark man; your brow
Is heavier than the night.
Away, away! Come, Harold, now.
And end my woman's fright!"

"Cry louder, Queen; your voice must rend
The grave, or find instead

The trump of doom if you would send
A message to the dead.

"An hour we fought; the fight was hot —
I flung away the sheath:
Here on my sword his blood lies cold;
His corpse, upon the heath."

"Why did you this?" "For love of you."
"Then with your wicked sword
Mix my life's flood with that sweet blood
Of him my soul adored."

"Not so; I did your people's will:
Now you must be my wife."
"What! murder on my heart's door-sill
My only love, my life,

"Then rouse up with your bloody sword
The love you have bereft,
And straight demand my heart and hand!
Is there no lightning left?

"My Queen, I saw his thievish glance,
The untimely smile, the fear;
I saw his vision like a lance
Pierce him who had your ear.

"I marked him gaze till he could feast
His eyes your eyes upon,
Like that ecstatic orient priest
Who watches for the dawn.

"And when your whisper blessed his ears,
I saw his soul rejoice,
Like some far traveller who hears
The dusky Memnon's voice.

"And when your hand touched his for joy,
Or in the press by luck
Blown like a lily, I saw the boy
Reel like one lightning-struck.

"And when your breath of Eastern spice — "
"O God, give o'er!" cried she.
"Such sights," he said, "would melt raw ice
To fiery jealousy.

"What more? I struck young Harold dead
In fair fight at a stone.
Whereon I laid his golden head;
And there he lies alone.

"Two streams meet there and softly prate
Of all their wandering ways,
Like children when their hearts are great
With deeds of holidays.

"They heeded not when we two fought;
They heed not that pale lord — "
"Is it his blood that wanders there
Upon your dreadful sword?"

She took the sword; it made her reel;
Her tears came in a flood;
They fell upon the ruddy steel,
And mingled with the blood.

Then with her raven hair she wiped
The tear-drenched blood away;
A moonbeam strayed along the blade,
And left it cold and gray.

"Now, hell-brand, do your work!" she cried.
And ran him through and through.
The sword stood quivering in his side.
But still his breath came true.

"Prince, are you dead?'' she hoarsely said.
He smiled upon the Queen:
"No, I am dying for your love.
As I have always been;

"So, give me now your hand to kiss,"
She gave the Prince her hand.
"This steel is cold; take, now, good hold.
And pluck away the brand."

John Davidson – A Short Biography

John Davidson was born at Barrhead, East Renfrewshire on 11th April 1857, the son of Alexander Davidson, an Evangelical Union minister and Helen née Crocket of Elgin.

In 1862 the family moved to Greenock and Davidson began his education at Highlanders' Academy. From there he began his career, aged a mere 13, at the chemical laboratory of Walker's Sugarhouse refinery. A year later he returned to Highlander's, this time as a pupil teacher.

During his later employment at the Public Analysts' Office, 1870–71 he developed a keen interest in science which later became an important characteristic of his poetry. He returned once again to the Highlander's Academy, this time for four years, in 1872, again as a pupil teacher. In 1876 he spent a year at Edinburgh University before his first scholastic employment at Alexander's Charity, Glasgow which led to short periods of employment at various other schools over the following half a dozen years.

This led to a stint at Morrison's Academy in Crieff (1885–88), and in a private school at Greenock (1888–89).

In 1885 Davidson married Margaret McArthur and the marriage produced two children, Alexander (born in 1887) and Menzies (born in 1889).

Davidson's first published work was 'Bruce, A Chronicle Play', written in the Elizabethan style, and published by a local Glasgow imprint in 1886. Four other plays quickly followed; 'Smith, A Tragic Farce' (1888), 'An Unhistorical Pastoral' (1889), 'A Romantic Farce' (1889), and then the somewhat brilliant pantomime 'Scaramouch in Naxos' (1889).

By now he was very much immersed in literature and, in 1889, he ventured to London where he frequented the famous Fleet Street pub 'Ye Olde Cheshire Cheese' and joined the 'Rhymers' Club', a poets group that was based there.

Davidson was a prolific and hard-working writer. As well as his plays he wrote for the Speaker, the Glasgow Herald, and several other papers. He also wrote and had published several novels and tales, with perhaps the best being 'Perfervid' (1890).

With his reputation gradually providing an income he was also able to explore his true medium; Verse. 'In a Music Hall and Other Poems' (1891) together with 'Fleet Street Eclogues' (1893) were ample proof that he possessed a quite rare, genuine and distinctive poetic gift. Praise came from his peers including George Gissing and WB Yeats who wrote that it was: 'An example of a new writer seeking out new subject matter, new emotions'.

Davidson now turned further and further towards verse. In 1894 he published his most popular volume, 'Ballads and Songs' (1894), and this was followed by a further 'Fleet Street Eclogues' (Second Series) (1896) and by 'New Ballads' (1897) and 'The Last Ballad' (1899).

Davidson was a prolific writer. Besides the works cited, he wrote many other works including, 'The Wonderful Mission of Earl Lavender' (1895), a novel which extends his literary canon to flagellation erotica. He also contributed an introduction to Shakespeare's Sonnets (Renaissance edition, 1908), which, like his various prefaces and essays, shows him to be a subtle literary critic.

As the new century dawned Davidson was hard at work on a series of 'Testaments', in which he gave definite expression to his philosophy and these were published over a seven year period; 'The Testament of a Vivisector' (1901), 'The Testament of a Man Forbid' (1901), 'The Testament of an Empire Builder' (1902), and 'The Testament of John Davidson' (1908).

Though he played down any thought of himself as a philosopher, he expounded an original philosophy which was at once materialistic and aristocratic.

His later verse, which is often fine rhetoric rather than poetry, expressed his belief which is summed up in the last words that he wrote, "Men are the universe become conscious; the simplest man should consider himself too great to be called after any name." Davidson professed to reject all existing philosophies, including that of Nietzsche, as inadequate. The poet planned to expand and expound on his revolutionary creed in a trilogy entitled 'God and Mammon'. Only two plays, however, were written, 'The Triumph of Mammon' (1907) and 'Mammon and his Message' (1908).

In addition to his own work Davidson was a noted translator of other works which included Montesquieu's 'Lettres Persanes' (1892), François Coppée's 'Pour la Couronne' in 1896 and Victor Hugo's 'Ruy Blas' in 1904, the former being produced as, 'For the Crown', at the Lyceum Theatre in 1896, the latter as 'A Queen's Romance' at the Imperial Theatre.

Frank Harris, a member of the Rhymers' Club and himself a writer of erotic literature described him in 1889 as: "... a little below middle height, but strongly built with square shoulders and remarkably fine face and head; the features were almost classically regular, the eyes dark brown and large, the forehead high, the hair and moustache black. His manners were perfectly frank and natural; he met everyone in the same unaffected kindly human way; I never saw a trace in him of snobbishness or incivility. Possibly a great man, I said to myself, certainly a man of genius, for simplicity of manner alone is in England almost a proof of extraordinary endowment."

In 1906 he was awarded a civil list pension of £100 per annum and George Bernard Shaw did what he could to help him financially. However other issues were also circling besides poverty. Ill-health, and his declining intellectual powers, amplified by the onset of cancer, caused profound hopelessness and clinical depression.

Late in 1908, Davidson left London to live in Penzance in Cornwall. On 23rd March 1909, he left his house and was not seen again. There seemed no sound reason not to believe that he had done so with the intention of drowning himself. On an examination of his office a new manuscript was found. It was a poetry book; 'Fleet Street Poems', with a letter bleakly stating confirming, "This will be my last book."

Indeed in his philosophic book 'The Testament of John Davidson', published the year before his death, he anticipates this fate:

"None should outlive his power. . . . Who kills
Himself subdues the conqueror of kings;
Exempt from death is he who takes his life;
My time has come."

Davidson's body was not discovered until 18th September in Mount's cave by some fishermen. In accordance with his will it was now buried at sea. Strangely it seemed Davidson's wish that none of his unpublished works, nor any biography be published and "no word except of my writing is ever to appear in any book of mine as long as the copyright endures."

Davidson's poetry was a key early influence on important Modernist poets, in particular, his compatriot Hugh MacDiarmid, Wallace Stevens and T.S. Eliot.

John Davidson – A Concise Bibliography

The North Wall (1885)
Diabolus Amans (1885) Verse drama
Bruce (1886) A drama in five acts
Smith (1888) A tragedy
An Unhistorical Pastoral, A Romantic Farce (1889)
Scaramouch in Naxos (1889)
Perfervid: The Career of Ninian Jamieson (1890) with 23 Original Illustrations by Harry Furniss
The Great Men, And a Practical Novelist (1891) Illustrated by E. J. Ellis.
In a Music Hall, and other Poems (1891)
Laura Ruthven's Widowhood (with C. J. Wills) (1892)
Fleet Street Eclogues (1893)
The Knight of the Maypole, (1903)
Sentences and Paragraphs (1893)
Ballads and Songs (1894)
Baptist Lake (1894)
A Random Itinerary (1894)
A Full and True Account of the Wonderful Mission of Earl Lavender (1895)
St. George's Day (1895)
Fleet Street Eclogues (Second Series) (1896)
Miss Armstrong's and Other Circumstances (1896)
The Pilgrimage of Strongsoul and Other Stories (1896)
New Ballads (1897)
Godfrida, a play (1898)
The Last Ballad (1899)
Self's the Man, A tragi-comedy (1901)
The Testament of a Man Forbid (1901)
The Testament of a Vivisector (1901)
The Testament of an Empire Builder (1902)
A Rosary (1903)
The Knight of the Maypole: A Comedy in Four Acts (1903)
The Testament of a Prime Minister (1904) [7]
The Ballad of a Nun (1905)
The Theatrocrat: A Tragic Play of Church and State (1905)
Holiday and other poems, with a note on poetry (1906)
The Triumph of Mammon (1907)
Mammon and His Message (1908)
The Testament of John Davidson (1908)
Fleet Street and other Poems (1909)

He was also a contributor to 'The Yellow Book' periodical

As Translator

Montesquieu's Lettres Persanes (Persian Letters) (1892)
François Coppée's Pour la couronne (For the Crown) (1896)
Victor Hugo's Ruy Blas (A Queen's Romance) (1904)

www.ingramcontent.com/pod-product-compliance
Lightning Source LLC
Chambersburg PA
CBHW021942040426
42448CB00008B/1193